Profiles of the Presidents

DWIGHT D. EISENHOWER

★ ★ ★

Profiles of the Presidents

DWIGHT D. EISENHOWER

by Lucia Raatma

Content Adviser: Harry Rubenstein, Curator of Political History Collections, National Museum of American History, Smithsonian Institution
Reading Adviser: Dr. Linda D. Labbo, Department of Reading Education, College of Education, The University of Georgia

COMPASS POINT BOOKS ✦ MINNEAPOLIS, MINNESOTA

Compass Point Books
151 Good Counsel Drive
P. O. Box 669
Mankato, MN 56002-0669

Visit Compass Point Books on the Internet at *www.compasspointbooks.com*
or e-mail your request to *custserv@compasspointbooks.com*

Photographs ©: Hulton/Archive by Getty Images, cover, 3, 7, 16, 17, 18, 20, 22, 23, 27, 30, 31, 33, 39 (right), 41, 42, 44, 45, 47, 54 (right), 55 (right), 58 (right), 59 (right); Bettmann/Corbis, 6, 24, 29, 32, 35, 37, 38 (top), 49, 56 (left), 57 (top left), 59 (top left); Dwight D. Eisenhower Library, 8, 10, 11, 12, 13, 15, 54 (bottom left), 55 (left); Philip Gould/Corbis, 9, 54 (top left); Stock Montage, 14, 19, 21, 25, 28, 34, 38 (bottom), 57 (bottom left), 58 (top left); NASA Kennedy Space Center, 39 (left); DigitalVision, 40; Corbis, 43, 58 (bottom left); James L. Amos/Corbis, 50, 59 (bottom left); Franklin D. Roosevelt Library, 56 (left); Galen Rowell/Corbis, 57 (right).

Editors: E. Russell Primm, Emily J. Dolbear, Melissa McDaniel, and Catherine Neitge
Photo Researcher: Svetlana Zhurkina
Photo Selector: Linda S. Koutris
Designer: The Design Lab
Cartographer: XNR Productions, Inc.

Library of Congress Cataloging-in-Publication Data

Raatma, Lucia.
  Dwight D. Eisenhower / by Lucia Raatma.
     v. cm. — (Profiles of the presidents)
Includes bibliographical references and index.
Contents: "Little Ike"—Rising in the ranks—A leader in war—In the nation's highest office—The challenges of a second term—The end of a memorable life.
  ISBN 13: 978-0-7565-0279-9
  ISBN 10: 0-7565-0279-9
  1. Eisenhower, Dwight D. (Dwight David), 1890–1969—Juvenile literature. 2. Presidents—United States—Biography—Juvenile literature. 3. United States—Politics and government—1953–1961—Juvenile literature. [1. Eisenhower, Dwight D. (Dwight David), 1890–1969. 2. Presidents.] I. Title. II. Series.
  E836 .R25 2002
  973.921'092—dc21   2002003013

Printed in the United States of America.

Table of Contents

★ ★ ★

"I Like Ike!"

★ ★ ★

"**I** Like Ike!" That was the **slogan** on many buttons and posters when Dwight David Eisenhower was running for president in 1952. Most of the American public agreed with the slogan. Eisenhower won the election and became the thirty-fourth president of the United States.

At that time, Eisenhower was not known for being a politician. He had been a military hero during World War II (1939–1945), leading the Allied forces in Europe to victory.

*A campaign ▶
license plate
attachment sporting
the popular slogan*

I LIKE
IKE

◀ General Eisen-
hower, always
a friend to the
troops, talks
with one of his
soldiers during
World War II.

When he became president, he committed himself to keeping peace. Late in his presidency, he remarked, "The United States never lost a soldier or a foot of ground in my administration. We kept the peace. People asked how it happened—by God, it didn't *just* happen, I'll tell you that."

Americans had suffered through war and economic hard times in the years before Eisenhower was elected. They were ready for peace and **prosperity**. Eisenhower gave them just that.

Little Ike

★ ★ ★

David Dwight Eisenhower was born on October 14, 1890, in Denison, Texas. Throughout his life, he was called Dwight. At some point, his names were reversed to Dwight David. His parents, David Jacob Eisenhower

◄ The Eisenhower
family in 1902
(Dwight is on the
far left.)

and Ida Stover Eisenhower, had six other sons— Arthur, Edgar, Roy, Earl, and Milton, as well as Paul, who died when he was a baby. The family was very religious.

▲ *Eisenhower's boyhood home in Abilene, Kansas, now houses the Eisenhower Center.*

They belonged to the River Brethren, a Protestant group. The Eisenhowers read the Bible every day and often prayed together. Dwight remained religious throughout his life, joining the Presbyterian Church as an adult.

Edgar Eisenhower was often called Big Ike, while his younger brother Dwight was called Little Ike. This nickname became just Ike when Dwight was an adult.

All the Eisenhower boys learned to work hard as they were growing up. Dwight spent most of his childhood in Abilene, Kansas, where the family moved when he was less than two years old. His father worked for a business that made butter and cheese. Dwight and his brothers tended chickens and cows on the family farm. They also grew vegetables, which the family sold for extra money.

In school, Dwight was an average student, but he loved sports. He played both baseball and football. As a young man, he also had a bad temper. He sometimes got into fights or got upset when things did not go his way. With the help of his mother, however, he learned to

The 1909 Abilene High School baseball team (Dwight is fourth from left, front row.) ▼

control himself.
Coming to terms
with his temper
proved very impor-
tant later in his life
when the world
depended on him
for peace.

Both Dwight
and Edgar were
eager to go to col-

*Dwight D. Eisen-
hower at age
twenty-five in his
cadet uniform*

lege. The Eisenhowers, however, did not have the money
to send their sons to expensive universities. So Dwight
and Edgar found a solution. Dwight agreed that after
high school he would work full time with his father and
send money to Edgar for college. Then Edgar would
take a year off and do the same for Dwight. At first, the
plan worked.

Then a friend of Dwight's told him that military
schools in the United States were free. Dwight didn't real-
ly want to be a soldier, but he liked the idea of a free education. So he studied for the entrance exams for the U.S.
Naval Academy at Annapolis, Maryland, and the U.S.

Eisenhower (second from the left) was a member of the 1912 West Point football team.

Military Academy at West Point, New York. After passing both exams, he found out that, at age twenty, he was too old to go to Annapolis. So he set off for West Point.

At West Point, Dwight Eisenhower played on the army football team. A knee injury forced him to leave the team, however. As when he was younger, Dwight was still an average student, but he worked as hard as he could. When he graduated from the academy in 1915, he ranked 61st out of the 164 members in the class.

Rising in the Ranks

★ ★ ★

After graduation, Eisenhower was made a second lieutenant and assigned to Fort Sam Houston in Texas. During his time there, he met Mamie Doud, a young woman who was visiting the army base. They began dating, and soon their relationship became serious. On July 1, 1916, Dwight Eisenhower and Mamie Doud were married. The couple had two sons. Doud Dwight, who was

▲ *Dwight and Mamie Eisenhower on their wedding day*

Mamie Eisenhower ▲
with her second
son, John

born in 1917, died at age three from scarlet fever. John Sheldon Doud was born in 1922 and went on to become an army officer.

On the same day that he was married, Eisenhower was promoted to first lieutenant. The following year, the United States entered World War I (1914–1918). By that time, Eisenhower had become known as a solid leader with good organizational skills. He was promoted to captain and assigned to Camp Colt in Gettysburg, Pennsylvania.

In Pennsylvania, Eisenhower taught soldiers how to use tanks in battle. He was a good teacher, but he wanted to see combat. His group was just about to ship out to France when the war ended. Eisenhower was disappointed that he didn't get to fight in the war. The officers above Eisenhower were very impressed with him, however, and he was awarded the Distinguished Service Medal.

After the war, Eisenhower moved to Camp Meade in Maryland, where he continued to specialize in tank **tactics**. Then, in 1922, Eisenhower was sent to the Panama Canal Zone, in Central America. There he served on the staff of Brigadier General Fox Connor, a

◄ *Eisenhower with the Tank Corps at Camp Meade*

John J. Pershing ▲

man who influenced Eisenhower greatly. Connor taught Eisenhower about military history and **strategies.**

With Connor's encouragement, the next year Eisenhower went to Fort Leavenworth, Kansas, to attend the Command and General Staff School. The officers there studied military skills. It was a very competitive school, but Eisenhower was inspired by what he was learning. He finished at the top of his class.

Dwight Eisenhower's performance at the Command and General Staff School caught the attention of key army leaders. One was General John J. Pershing. He was heading a commission that was overseeing U.S. war memorials in France. Eisenhower became his aide. Then, in 1928, Eisenhower enrolled in the Army War College. The following year, he again graduated at the top of his class.

Another important leader who had heard about Eisenhower was General Douglas MacArthur, the army chief of staff. In 1933, MacArthur appointed Eisenhower as his

▲ *General Douglas MacArthur*

aide. Later, Eisenhower was named MacArthur's chief of staff. In 1935, MacArthur became a military adviser to the Philippines. MacArthur and Eisenhower traveled to this group of Asian islands. There they helped the government build a strong army and prepared the nation for independence. Eisenhower stayed in the Philippines for four years. By the time he left, he had been promoted to lieutenant colonel.

A Leader in War

★ ★ ★

In 1939, World War II began in Europe. The Axis powers, which included Germany, Italy, and Japan, fought the Allied forces, which included France, Great Britain, and

Adolf Hitler and his Nazi Party led Germany into war. ▾

later the Soviet
Union. The
United States did
not get involved in
the war at first,
but many people
thought the coun-
try would be
drawn in later.
With that in
mind, the United
States began
preparing for war.

▲ *General George*
C. Marshall

In 1941, Eis-
enhower helped lead a series of war games being held in
Louisiana. These "games" helped teach troops how to
plan strategy for war. Eisenhower performed well and
again caught the attention of army leaders, including
General George C. Marshall, the army chief of staff.

On December 7, 1941, Japanese fighter planes
attacked a U.S. naval base at Pearl Harbor in Hawaii.
This violent act forced the United States to enter the
war and give its full support to the Allied efforts.

Dwight Eisenhower (right) and American general George Patton discuss the invasion of North Africa.

General Marshall named Dwight Eisenhower as head of the War Plans Division.

In June 1942, Eisenhower was put in charge of U.S. forces in Europe. That November, he led an Allied invasion of North Africa. It was a success, and he was promoted to general. He went on to lead invasions in Italy. He became very successful at getting leaders of different nations to work together as a team.

As the war continued, U.S. president Franklin D. Roosevelt and British prime minister Winston Churchill worked together closely. They helped devise a plan to invade European areas that were **occupied** by German troops. In December 1943, Roosevelt put Eisenhower in charge of that invasion, which was called Operation Overlord. Eisenhower became the supreme commander of all Allied forces in Europe.

The plan of Operation Overlord was to have troops leave England, cross the English Channel, and land on the beaches of Normandy in northern France. Eisenhower spent months planning the attack. The success of the invasion depended on good weather and low tides.

On June 6, 1944, Operation Overlord began. It was the largest seaborne invasion in history. June 6 became known as D-Day. In the coming weeks, Allied troops pushed the German troops back. Finally, France was secure. This was a major

▼ *Franklin D. Roosevelt and Winston Churchill met often. The United States and Great Britain became great friends and allies during World War II.*

U.S. fleets bring supplies and troops to the beaches of Normandy a month after the Allied invasion on June 6, 1944.

victory for the Allies. By the end of the year, Eisenhower had been promoted to five-star general, a new rank in the U.S. Army.

But the war was not over yet. Fighting continued in Europe for almost another year. The Battle of the Bulge in December 1944 was Germany's last important **offensive.** Many Allied leaders were depressed by the German success in that battle. Eisenhower showed remarkable leadership, however. He inspired the troops and helped the leaders of the Allied forces to work together. As a result, Germany **surrendered,** on May 7, 1945.

After the Allied victory, General Marshall sent Eisenhower a message that read in part, "You have completed your mission with the greatest victory in the history of warfare. . . . You have been selfless in your actions, always sound and tolerant in your judgments and altogether admirable in the courage and wisdom of your military decisions."

Japan surrendered in August 1945, ending World War II. After the war, Eisenhower served as army chief of staff. In 1948, he published *Crusade in Europe,* a book about his experiences in World War II. That same year, he became

◀ *Field Marshall Wilhelm Keitel signs the surrender terms for the German army in Berlin.*

Dwight D. ▶
Eisenhower was
briefly the
president of
Columbia
University.

president of Columbia University in New York City. But
soon he would again be asked to serve his country.

In 1922, Russia and other nations in eastern Europe
and central Asia had combined to form the Soviet Union.
The Soviet Union worked under a system called **communism**, in which the government controlled nearly every-
thing. In the following years, other countries in eastern
Europe also became communist. This caused growing
tension between the United States and the Soviet Union.

★

The two nations began competing for power around the world. This competition was known as the Cold War.

President Harry S. Truman was worried that communism might spread to western Europe. To stop that from happening, the United States and many western European nations formed the North Atlantic Treaty Organization (NATO) in 1950. Truman chose Eisenhower to command NATO forces.

In the meantime, North Korea, which was communist, had invaded South Korea, and the Korean War (1950–1953) had begun. U.S. troops were sent to help South Korea. Once again, the United States was at war.

◀ *Eisenhower meets with U.S. president Harry Truman.*

In the Nation's Highest Office

★ ★ ★

As the 1952 presidential election drew nearer, leaders of both the Republican and the Democratic parties had their eyes on General Dwight D. Eisenhower. He was the most popular hero of World War II, and leaders around the world respected him. Either party would have been happy to have him as their **candidate** for president.

Eisenhower had never believed that soldiers should run for political office. Yet, as politicians argued about the Korean War, Eisenhower began to change his mind. Senator Robert Taft of Ohio was a leading Republican candidate for president. He believed that the United States should get out of Korea, and he did not think NATO should even exist. Eisenhower believed that the United States had a duty to help make the rest of the world a better place. Eisenhower came to believe that he could best serve his country as its president.

Dwight Eisenhower announced in April 1952 that he would run as a Republican for president of the United States. Voters were impressed by his leadership. They liked his warm personality and easy smile, too. He beat Robert Taft to become the Republican candidate. Richard Nixon, a U.S. senator from California, was asked to run for vice president.

▲ *Dwight D. Eisenhower with his running mate, Richard Nixon (center), and chairman of the Republican National Committee, Arthur Summerfield*

Adlai Stevenson, Democratic presidential candidate

The Democrats chose Adlai Stevenson, the governor of Illinois, to be their candidate for president. John Sparkman, a senator from Alabama, was the Democratic candidate for vice president.

During the summer and fall of 1952, Eisenhower campaigned across the country. He and his staff traveled on a train called *Look Ahead, Neighbor.* In towns all over America, people met the train and listened to Eisenhower speak. They waved "I Like Ike" banners and cheered at the end of his speeches. The public seemed to love the down-to-earth candidate and Mamie, his friendly wife.

On Election Day 1952, Eisenhower got 55 percent of the vote and defeated Stevenson 442 to 89 in the Electoral College. In that same election, Republicans gained control in both houses of Congress.

As president, Eisenhower surrounded himself with

Dwight and
Mamie
Eisenhower
campaign from
the back of a
train in Hastings,
Nebraska.

*Secretary of State ▲
John Foster Dulles*

intelligent, trustworthy advisers. He appointed John Foster Dulles as secretary of state, and he named George Humphrey as secretary of the treasury. Herbert Brownell Jr. became attorney general, and Charles E. Wilson was made secretary of defense.

Eisenhower became president at a time when the country was enjoying prosperity. After the terrible economic depression of the 1930s and World War II, Americans wanted to feel safe and comfortable again. With his easygoing manner, Eisenhower was the perfect leader for the times.

As president, Eisenhower worked with Congress to cut government spending on some programs that helped people in need. But he also worked to improve Social Security, the national program that helps the elderly and the disabled.

He supported a number of big projects that were meant to help the U.S. economy. Among these was the building of the St. Lawrence Seaway. This waterway

◄ *The construction of the St. Lawrence Seaway, which was completed in 1959*

allowed big ships to travel all the way from the Atlantic Ocean to the Great Lakes. Eisenhower also supported the creation of interstate highways. Work on this system of highways began in 1956. These roads greatly improved travel conditions from coast to coast.

Shortly after taking office, Eisenhower quickly moved to end the Korean War. A **truce** was signed in July 1953. His success was partly a result of his threat to use powerful weapons against the North Koreans. He believed that a big U.S. supply of nuclear weapons

A truce brought ▶
the end of the
Korean War but did
not stop the threat
of communism.

would prevent other countries from starting wars. In a
1956 radio address, he stated, "The only way to win
World War III is to prevent it."

At one point, Eisenhower had hoped to rid Europe
of communism. But after he became president, he real-
ized how hard that would be. So he settled for keeping

communism from spreading to other countries.

In the 1950s, many Americans believed that communism posed a threat to the United States. Beginning in 1950, Senator Joseph McCarthy of Wisconsin claimed that communists were working in the State Department and in the military. He had no proof, but he put fear into the minds of many Americans. McCarthy demanded to see government files that he said proved his claims were true. Eisenhower refused. Eisenhower did not like what McCarthy was doing, but he never criticized the senator in public. Instead, he simply ignored him. After a while, McCarthy's **witch-hunt** came to an end.

▼ *Senator McCarthy (right) fed on Americans' fear during the Cold War.*

In spite of his many successes during his first term, Eisenhower was not sure that he wanted to run for a second term. While on vacation in Colorado in 1955, he had a heart

attack. Within a month, he began working from the hospital, and he was back in his office by the end of the year. Doctors told him he would probably live for many years. They said he should have no trouble serving another term as president.

Still, Eisenhower was tempted to retire. At age sixty-five, he had a busy and stressful life. He traveled all over the country and around the world. Maybe it was time to slow down. He looked forward to playing golf and relaxing. He and Mamie had bought a farm in Gettysburg, Pennsylvania, in 1950, and he longed to settle there. The Republicans pushed Eisenhower to run for a second term. They believed in his abilities. They also knew he was popular with the American people. So Eisenhower agreed.

Once again he faced Democrat Adlai Stevenson in the election. He had an even stronger showing in his second election. This time he won 57 percent of the vote and received 457 electoral votes to Stevenson's 73.

▾ *The Eisenhower farm at Gettysburg was a place for the president to rest and recover.*

The Challenges of a Second Term

★ ★ ★

During his second term, President Eisenhower faced many challenges within the United States and around the world. At home, trying to enforce fair treatment for African-Americans was one of those challenges.

Throughout the South and in some other parts of the United States, laws kept black and white Americans

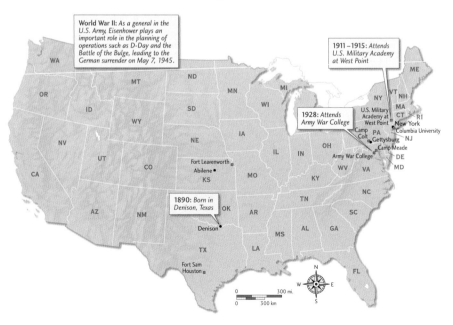

World War II: *As a general in the U.S. Army, Eisenhower plays an important role in the planning of operations such as D-Day and the Battle of the Bulge, leading to the German surrender on May 7, 1945.*

1911–1915: *Attends U.S. Military Academy at West Point*

1928: *Attends Army War College*

1890: *Born in Denison, Texas*

separate. Blacks were forced to go to different schools, sit in different sections of movie theaters, and even drink from different water fountains. This practice of separating blacks and whites was called segregation.

In 1954, the U.S. Supreme Court had ruled that segregation of public schools was **unconstitutional.** The court ordered all public schools to **integrate,** so that children of all races and backgrounds would attend class together. Eisenhower never said in public what

▼ *African-American children were sent to different schools from white children.*

he thought of this ruling. He didn't usually believe in making laws that would force social change. In 1957, he was put to the test, however.

In September, Governor Orval Faubus of Arkansas tried to stop the integration of Little Rock Central High School. He called in the state's

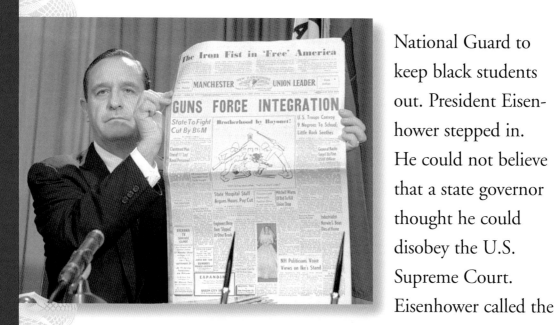

National Guard to keep black students out. President Eisenhower stepped in. He could not believe that a state governor thought he could disobey the U.S. Supreme Court. Eisenhower called the Arkansas National Guard into federal service. This meant that the troops had to follow his orders and not the governor's. He also sent army troops to Little Rock to keep the peace and to protect the African-American students. This was a very difficult time in U.S. history. Eisenhower did what was needed to enforce the laws and to prevent violence.

Governor Orval Faubus publicly attacked the president for using army troops to enforce integration and to protect black students.

The Cold War continued to dominate Eisenhower's second term. In the twentieth century, the United States had become a world leader in technology. So it came as a shock when the Soviet Union became the first nation to send an object into space. In October 1957, the Soviet Union launched a satellite named *Sputnik I* into orbit around Earth. The following January, the United States launched a satellite called *Explorer I.* The space race was on.

▾ *The Soviet Union's satellite* Sputnik I *(right) beat the American* Explorer I *(left) into space by only three months.*

Until that time, the military had been handling all missions into space, but there was no single agency to head the programs. So in 1958, Eisenhower signed a law creating the National Aeronautics and Space Administration (NASA). This agency oversees all space research and exploration. In the coming years, NASA had many great successes. One of its most memorable came in July 1969, when American astronaut Neil Armstrong became the first person to set foot on the Moon.

Moon landing! ▶
Apollo 11 *landed on the Moon on July 24, 1969.*

Much of Eisenhower's second term dealt with controlling the spread of communism. In 1957, Congress approved the Eisenhower Doctrine, which said that the United States would give money and military aid to any country fighting the spread of communism. Under this policy, the United States sent troops to Lebanon in July 1958. One month later, the United States sent supplies to islands governed by Taiwan. These islands were fighting the communist government of China.

◀ *U.S. Army tanks arrive in Beirut, Lebanon.*

Fidel Castro speaks to his supporters five days before entering Cuba's capital, Havana.

The following year, Fidel Castro came to power in Cuba. This island nation in the Caribbean Sea is only 90 miles (145 kilometers) from Florida. In 1960, Castro seized all land and buildings owned by U.S. companies in Cuba. Suddenly the threat of communism was very close to the United States.

In 1959, President Eisenhower had an important meeting with Nikita Khrushchev, the leader of the Soviet Union. This meeting marked the first time that a Soviet leader had visited the United States. Eisenhower was to meet with Khrushchev again the following year. Eisenhower hoped this meeting would improve relations between the United States and the Soviet Union.

▼ *Eisenhower and Khrushchev shook hands, but their good will was short-lived.*

Francis Gary Powers holds a model of the spy plane he was flying when his plane was shot down by the Soviet military. He was captured and then returned to the United States in exchange for a captured Soviet spy.

In May 1960, just before the meeting was to take place, the Soviet military shot down an American spy plane. Khrushchev demanded that the United States apologize for spying. Eisenhower refused. He blamed U.S. spying on Soviet secrecy. He said it was the only way the United States could be sure that the Soviet Union was not preparing an attack. The second meeting with Khrushchev never took place. In the years to come, relations between the United States and the Soviet Union became even more difficult.

As 1960 drew to a close, President Eisenhower prepared to leave office. Since the presidency was limited to two terms, he could not run again. He supported Vice President Richard Nixon in his campaign for the presidency. But a Democrat—John F. Kennedy—won the

▾ *Eisenhower's vice president, Richard Nixon (left), debated Democratic senator John F. Kennedy during the 1960 presidential campaign. It was the first televised presidential debate.*

election. Eisenhower was disappointed, but he met with Kennedy and gave him the best advice he could. He also warned him: "No easy matters will ever come to you . . . If they're easy, they will be settled at a lower level."

1953: *Helps to end the Korean War.*

1952: *Elected 34th president of the U.S*
1956: *Reelected to another four-year term*

1957–1958: *Protests erupt when Little Rock Central High School is integrated. Eisenhower federalizes the Arkansas National Guard, ordering them to protect the African-American students so that they can attend school.*

1958: *Creates NASA to help the U.S. compete in the "space race" against the Soviet Union.*

June 29, 1956: *Signs the Federal Aid Highway Act, laying the foundation for today's interstate highways, now known as the Eisenhower Interstate Highway System.*

1960: *U.S. imposes economic sanctions on Cuba to try to keep communism from taking hold.*

Eisenhower Presidential Center
Abilene

Little Rock

Gettysburg
Washington, D.C.

The End of a Memorable Life

★ ★ ★

In his farewell speech in January 1961, Dwight Eisenhower warned the United States of the dangers it faced. He said he believed the nation needed to build

▼ President Eisenhower greeted the nation's next president, John F. Kennedy, in 1960.

President Eisenhower greeted the nation's next president, John F. Kennedy, in 1960.

up the military—not to start a war, but to prevent one. He warned against being influenced by other powerful countries. He ended his speech with the hope that "all people will come to live together in a peace guaranteed by the binding force of mutual respect and love."

Once out of the White House, Dwight and Mamie Eisenhower retired to their Gettysburg farm and lived a more quiet life. President Eisenhower spent much of his time writing.

Occasionally, other presidents called him for advice. He spoke with President Kennedy about relations with Cuba. And he discussed the Vietnam War with President Lyndon Johnson. In 1968, Eisenhower supported Richard Nixon in his successful campaign for president. That same year, Nixon's daughter Julie married Dwight Eisenhower's grandson David Eisenhower.

Eisenhower's health had begun to fail in 1965. In the following years, he had three more heart attacks. Before his death on March 28, 1969, Eisenhower summed up his life this way: "I've always loved my wife. I've always loved my children. I've always loved my grandchildren. And I have always loved my country."

A full military funeral was held for Dwight David

◄ *Julie and David
Eisenhower on
their wedding day*

Eisenhower, the celebrated general, the respected leader, and the popular president. He was laid to rest at his family home in Abilene, Kansas.

Mourners gathered in Washington National Cathedral to say goodbye to Dwight Eisenhower. Mamie Eisenhower died ten years later in 1979.

GLOSSARY

★ ★ ★

candidate—someone running for office in an election

communism—an economic system in which all businesses are owned by the government

integrate—to make open to people of all races

occupied—took control of during a war

offensive—an attack during wartime

prosperity—economic well-being

slogan—a phrase used to capture public attention in a campaign

strategies—plans and methods used in war

surrendered—gave up

tactics—ways to use forces in combat

truce—an agreement to stop the fighting in a war

unconstitutional—not agreeing with the U.S. Constitution

witch-hunt—the search for and harassment of those with unpopular views

DWIGHT D. EISENHOWER'S LIFE AT A GLANCE

★ ★ ★

PERSONAL

Nickname:	Ike
Birth date:	October 14, 1890
Birthplace:	Denison, Texas
Father's name:	David Jacob Eisenhower
Mother's name:	Ida Elizabeth Stover Eisenhower
Education:	Graduated from the U.S. Military Academy at West Point, New York, in 1915
Wife's name:	Mamie Geneva Doud Eisenhower
Married:	July 1, 1916
Children:	Doud Dwight Eisenhower (1917–1921); John Sheldon Doud Eisenhower (1922–)
Died:	March 28, 1969, in Washington, D.C.
Buried:	The Eisenhower Center, Abilene, Kansas

PUBLIC

Occupation before presidency:	Soldier
Occupation after presidency:	Statesman, author
Military service:	General of U.S. forces in Europe (1942–1943) and supreme commander of the Allied forces in Europe (1943–1945); army chief of staff (1945–1948); supreme commander of NATO forces (1950)
Political party:	Republican
Vice president:	Richard M. Nixon (1953–1961)
Dates in office:	January 20, 1953–January 20, 1961
Presidential opponent:	Governor Adlai E. Stevenson (Democrat), 1952 and 1956
Number of votes (Electoral College):	33,936,137 of 61,250,786 (442 of 531), 1952; 35,585,245 of 61,615,417 (457 of 531), 1956
Writings:	*Crusade in Europe* (1948); *Mandate for Change* (1965); *The White House Years,* (2 vols., 1963–1965); *Waging Peace* (1966); *At Ease: Stories I Tell to Friends* (1967)

★

Dwight D. Eisenhower's Cabinet

Secretary of state:
John Foster Dulles (1953–1959)
Christian A. Herter (1959–1961)

Secretary of the treasury:
George M. Humphrey (1953–1957)
Robert B. Anderson (1957–1961)

Secretary of defense:
Charles E. Wilson (1953–1957)
Neil H. McElroy (1957–1959)
Thomas S. Gates Jr. (1960–1961)

Attorney general:
Herbert Brownell Jr. (1953–1957)
William P. Rogers (1957–1961)

Postmaster general:
Arthur E. Summerfield (1953–1961)

Secretary of the interior:
Douglas J. McKay (1953–1956)
Frederick A. Seaton (1956–1961)

Secretary of agriculture:
Ezra Taft Benson (1953–1961)

Secretary of commerce:
Sinclair Weeks (1953–1958)
Lewis Strauss (1958–1959)
Frederick H. Mueller (1959–1960)

Secretary of labor:
Martin P. Durkin (1953)
James P. Mitchell (1953–1961)

Secretary of health, education, and welfare:
Oveta Culp Hobby (1953–1955)
Marion B. Folsom (1955–1958)
Arthur S. Flemming (1958–1961)

DWIGHT D. EISENHOWER'S LIFE AND TIMES

★   ★   ★

EISENHOWER'S LIFE		WORLD EVENTS

EISENHOWER'S LIFE

David Dwight Eisenhower is born on October 14 in Denison, Texas — 1890

1890

Family moves to Abilene, Kansas — 1891

Graduates from high school — 1909

WORLD EVENTS

1891 — The Roman Catholic Church publishes the encyclical *Rerum Novarum,* which supports the rights of labor

1899 — Isadora Duncan (right), one of the founders of modern dance, makes her debut in Chicago

1900

1909 — The National Association for the Advancement of Colored People (NAACP) is founded

EISENHOWER'S LIFE				WORLD EVENTS

1910

			1913	Henry Ford begins to use standard assembly lines to produce automobiles

Graduates from West Point; is assigned to Fort Sam Houston in Texas — 1915

Marries Mamie Doud — 1916

			1916	German-born physicist Albert Einstein publishes his general theory of relativity

Becomes leader of the tank corps at Camp Meade, Maryland — 1919

1920 — 1920 American women get the right to vote

1923 French actress Sarah Bernhardt (below) dies

Graduates first in his class from the Command and General Staff School — 1926

Serves as aide to General John J. Pershing and works on American Battle Monuments Commission — 1927

Enters Army War College in Washington, D.C. — 1928

1929 The stock exchange collapses and severe economic depression sets in

1930 — 1930 Designs for the first jet engine are submitted to the Patent Office in Britain

Begins serving as aide to General Douglas MacArthur and later accompanies him to the Philippines — 1933

EISENHOWER'S LIFE

1940

The United States enters World War II; Eisenhower is named head of the War Plans Division — 1941

Leads an Allied invasion of North Africa — 1942

Is named the supreme commander of Allied forces in Europe — 1943

Leads the D-Day invasion of France; is promoted to five-star general — 1944

May 7, accepts the German surrender — 1945

Becomes president of Columbia University — 1948

WORLD EVENTS

1941 — December 7, Japanese bombers attack Pearl Harbor, Hawaii

1944 — DNA (deoxyribonucleic acid) is found to be the basis of heredity

1945 — America drops atomic bombs on Japanese cities of Hiroshima and Nagasaki to end World War II

The United Nations is founded

1949 — Birth of the People's Republic of China

EISENHOWER'S LIFE

Is appointed supreme commander of the North Atlantic Treaty Organization (NATO) forces — 1950

Is elected president — 1952

Helps end the Korean War — 1953

Suffers a heart attack — 1955

WORLD EVENTS

1950

Presidential Election Results:		Popular Votes	Electoral Votes
1952	Dwight D. Eisenhower	33,936,137	442
	Adlai E. Stevenson	27,314,649	89

1953 — The first Europeans climb Mount Everest (below)

EISENHOWER'S LIFE

| | WORLD EVENTS |

Is reelected president
of the United States — 1956

Presidential Election Results:		Popular Votes	Electoral Votes
1956	Dwight D. Eisenhower	35,585,245	457
	Adlai E. Stevenson	26,030,172	73
	Walter B. Jones		1

Sends troops
to oversee the
integration of
Little Rock
Central High
School (left) — 1957

Signs legislation to
create NASA — 1958

1958 — The Guggenheim
Museum in New York
opens

Hosts Soviet leader
Nikita Khrushchev
(below, far right) in
Washington, D.C. — 1959

1959 — Fidel Castro (below)
becomes prime
minister of Cuba

EISENHOWER'S LIFE

1960 Refuses to apologize for a U.S. spy plane that was in Soviet airspace

1961 Retires to Gettysburg, Pennsylvania

WORLD EVENTS

1960

1961 Soviet cosmonaut Yuri Gagarin (right) becomes first person to travel in space

1962 Rachel Carson's influential book *Silent Spring* is published, increasing environmental awareness nationwide

1968 Grandson marries Richard Nixon's daughter

1968 Civil rights leader Martin Luther King Jr. (above) is shot and killed.

1969 March 28, dies in Washington, D.C.

1969 U.S. astronauts are the first humans to land on the Moon

UNDERSTANDING DWIGHT D. EISENHOWER AND HIS PRESIDENCY

★ ★ ★

IN THE LIBRARY

Brown, Clayton D. *Dwight D. Eisenhower.*
Berkeley Heights, N.J.: Enslow, 1998.

Hargrove, Jim. *Dwight D. Eisenhower: Thirty-Fourth President of the
United States.* Chicago: Childrens Press, 1987.

Jacobs, William Jay. *Dwight David Eisenhower: Soldier and Statesman.*
New York: Franklin Watts, 1995.

Joseph, Paul. *Dwight D. Eisenhower.* Minneapolis:
Abdo and Daughters, 1999.

Lindop, Edmund. *Dwight D. Eisenhower, John F. Kennedy, and
Lyndon B. Johnson.* New York: Twenty-First Century Books, 1996.

Sinnott, Susan. *Mamie Doud Eisenhower.* Danbury, Conn.:
Children's Press, 2000.

ON THE WEB

For more information on *Dwight D. Eisenhower,* use
FactHound to track down Web sites related to this book.

1. Go to *www.facthound.com*
2. Type in this book ID: 0756502799
3. Click on the *Fetch It* button.

Your trusty FactHound will fetch the best Web sites for you!

EISENHOWER HISTORIC SITES
ACROSS THE COUNTRY

**Eisenhower National
Historic Site**
97 Taneytown Road
Gettysburg, PA 17325
717/338-9114
To visit the home of Dwight and
Mamie Eisenhower

**Eisenhower Birthplace State
Historic Park**
208 East Day
Denison, TX 75020
903/465-8908
To see where Eisenhower
was born

Eisenhower's Library & Museum
200 Southeast Fourth Street
Abilene, KS 67410
785/263-4751
877/RING-IKE
To visit Eisenhower's grave and a
museum dedicated to his life

THE U.S. PRESIDENTS
(Years in Office)

★ ★ ★

1. George Washington
   (March 4, 1789-March 3, 1797)
2. John Adams
   (March 4, 1797-March 3, 1801)
3. Thomas Jefferson
   (March 4, 1801-March 3, 1809)
4. James Madison
   (March 4, 1809-March 3, 1817)
5. James Monroe
   (March 4, 1817-March 3, 1825)
6. John Quincy Adams
   (March 4, 1825-March 3, 1829)
7. Andrew Jackson
   (March 4, 1829-March 3, 1837)
8. Martin Van Buren
   (March 4, 1837-March 3, 1841)
9. William Henry Harrison
   (March 6, 1841-April 4, 1841)
10. John Tyler
    (April 6, 1841-March 3, 1845)
11. James K. Polk
    (March 4, 1845-March 3, 1849)
12. Zachary Taylor
    (March 5, 1849-July 9, 1850)
13. Millard Fillmore
    (July 10, 1850-March 3, 1853)
14. Franklin Pierce
    (March 4, 1853-March 3, 1857)
15. James Buchanan
    (March 4, 1857-March 3, 1861)
16. Abraham Lincoln
    (March 4, 1861-April 15, 1865)
17. Andrew Johnson
    (April 15, 1865-March 3, 1869)

18. Ulysses S. Grant
    (March 4, 1869-March 3, 1877)
19. Rutherford B. Hayes
    (March 4, 1877-March 3, 1881)
20. James Garfield
    (March 4, 1881-Sept 19, 1881)
21. Chester Arthur
    (Sept 20, 1881-March 3, 1885)
22. Grover Cleveland
    (March 4, 1885-March 3, 1889)
23. Benjamin Harrison
    (March 4, 1889-March 3, 1893)
24. Grover Cleveland
    (March 4, 1893-March 3, 1897)
25. William McKinley
    (March 4, 1897-
    September 14, 1901)
26. Theodore Roosevelt
    (September 14, 1901-
    March 3, 1909)
27. William Howard Taft
    (March 4, 1909-March 3, 1913)
28. Woodrow Wilson
    (March 4, 1913-March 3, 1921)
29. Warren G. Harding
    (March 4, 1921-August 2, 1923)
30. Calvin Coolidge
    (August 3, 1923-March 3, 1929)
31. Herbert Hoover
    (March 4, 1929-March 3, 1933)
32. Franklin D. Roosevelt
    (March 4, 1933-April 12, 1945)

33. Harry S. Truman
    (April 12, 1945-
    January 20, 1953)
34. Dwight D. Eisenhower
    (January 20, 1953-
    January 20, 1961)
35. John F. Kennedy
    (January 20, 1961-
    November 22, 1963)
36. Lyndon B. Johnson
    (November 22, 1963-
    January 20, 1969)
37. Richard M. Nixon
    (January 20, 1969-
    August 9, 1974)
38. Gerald R. Ford
    (August 9, 1974-
    January 20, 1977)
39. James Earl Carter
    (January 20, 1977-
    January 20, 1981)
40. Ronald Reagan
    (January 20, 1981-
    January 20, 1989)
41. George H. W. Bush
    (January 20, 1989-
    January 20, 1993)
42. William Jefferson Clinton
    (January 20, 1993-
    January 20, 2001)
43. George W. Bush
    (January 20, 2001-)

INDEX

★ ★ ★

ABOUT THE AUTHOR

Lucia Raatma received her bachelor's degree in English literature from the University of South Carolina and her master's degree in cinema studies from New York University. She has written a wide range of books for young people. When she is not researching or writing, she enjoys going to movies, playing tennis, practicing yoga, and spending time with her husband, daughter, and golden retriever. She lives in New York.